MW00885087

PEOPLE

of the

BIBLE

A weekly reading and journal schedule for kids.

People of the Bible: A weekly reading and journal schedule for kids.

Copyright © by Ashley Dufe

Cover design by Shannon Klare

Find Ashley here:

Blog: myhousefullofboys.com

Facebook: myhousefullboys

Instagram: myhousefullofboysblog

This daily bible reading guide and journal for Kids is a great way to encourage and motivate Kids (and adults) of all ages to be intentional about digging deeper into the stories of the people of the Bible.

Each week will include a memory verse and 5 days worth of suggested scriptures that follow part of the life of one of the people of the Bible.

Following the weekly reading plan is a weekly weekend "wrap up," which will help your child remember what they read and focus on ways they can serve and pray for others. There is also a small section for them to draw the person or story with the intentions of being visual aid that will help your child better remember the story.

It is my prayer that this guide can be a blessing to children and their families as they set out to discover some of the great people of the Bible.

I would love for you to share this with your friends, families, and churches and leave me a review on Amazon.

-Ashley

WEEK 1

Adam and Eve

MEMORY VERSE
"So God created mankind in his own image, in the image of God he created them; male and female he created them."
-Genesis 1:27

☐ ## Day 1- Genesis 1:26-31
- What I learned _____
_____

☐ ## Day 2- Genesis 2:4-9; 15-25
- What I learned _____
_____

☐ ## Day 3- Genesis 3:1-13
- What I learned _____
_____

☐ ## Day 4- Genesis 3:14-24
- What I learned _____
_____

☐ ## Day 5- Genesis 4:1-16; 25-26
- What I learned _____
_____

WEEKEND WRAP UP

This week I will serve or share Jesus with...

_____

- Think of 3 Facts about our person of the week.
- How did God use this person?
- What can we learn from him/her?
- How can I apply their story to my own life?

THIS WEEK I'M PRAYING FOR...

_____
_____
_____
_____
_____
_____
_____

Draw what you think this person looked like.

WEEK 2

Noah

> ### MEMORY VERSE
> "By faith Noah, when warned about things not yet seen, in holy fear built an ark to save his family. By his faith he condemned the world and became heir of the righteousness that is in keeping with faith." -Hebrews 11:7

☐ ### Day 1- Genesis 6:5-22
- What I learned _____

_____

☐ ### Day 2- Genesis 7:1-10
- What I learned _____

_____

☐ ### Day 3- Genesis 7:11-24
- What I learned _____

_____

☐ ### Day 4- Genesis 8:1-22
- What I learned _____

_____

☐ ### Day 5- Genesis 9:1-17
- What I learned _____

_____

WEEKEND WRAP UP

This week I will serve or share Jesus with...

_____

- Think of 3 Facts about our person of the week.
- How did God use this person?
- What can we learn from him/her?
- How can I apply their story to my own life?

THIS WEEK I'M PRAYING FOR...

_____
_____
_____
_____
_____
_____
_____

Draw what you think this person looked like.

WEEK 3

Abraham

MEMORY VERSE
"I will surely bless you and make your descendants as numerous as the stars in the sky and the sand on the seashore." -Genesis 22:17

☐ **Day 1- Genesis 12:1-20**
- What I learned _____
  _____

☐ **Day 2- Genesis 15:1-21**
- What I learned _____
  _____

☐ **Day 3- Genesis 16:1-16**
- What I learned _____
  _____

☐ **Day 4- Genesis 21:1-21**
- What I learned _____
  _____

☐ **Day 5- Genesis 22:1-19**
- What I learned _____
  _____

WEEKEND WRAP UP

This week I will serve or share Jesus with...

_____

- Think of 3 Facts about our person of the week.
- How did God use this person?
- What can we learn from him/her?
- How can I apply their story to my own life?

THIS WEEK I'M PRAYING FOR...

_____
_____
_____
_____
_____
_____
_____

Draw what you think this person looked like.

WEEK 4

Isaac

MEMORY VERSE

"By faith Isaac blessed Jacob and Esau in regard to their future." -Hebrews 11:20

☐ ## Day 1- Genesis 24:1-31

- What I learned _____

_____

☐ ## Day 2- Genesis 24:32-58

- What I learned _____

_____

☐ ## Day 3- Genesis 25:19-34

- What I learned _____

_____

☐ ## Day 4- Genesis 27:1-24

- What I learned _____

_____

☐ ## Day 5- Genesis 27:25-40

- What I learned _____

_____

WEEKEND WRAP UP

This week I will serve or share Jesus with...

_____

- Think of 3 Facts about our person of the week.
- How did God use this person?
- What can we learn from him/her?
- How can I apply their story to my own life?

THIS WEEK I'M PRAYING FOR...

_____
_____
_____
_____
_____
_____
_____

Draw what you think this person looked like.

WEEK 5

Jacob

MEMORY VERSE
"Two nations are in your womb, and two peoples from within you will be separated; one people will be stronger than the other, and the older will serve the younger." -Genesis 25:23

☐ Day 1- Genesis 27:41-46; 28:1-9
- What I learned _____
_____

☐ Day 2- Genesis 28:10-22
- What I learned _____
_____

☐ Day 3- Genesis 29:1-14
- What I learned _____
_____

☐ Day 4- Genesis 29:15-30
- What I learned _____
_____

☐ Day 5- Genesis 30:25-43
- What I learned _____
_____

WEEKEND WRAP UP

This week I will serve or share Jesus with...

_____

- Think of 3 facts about our person of the week.
- How did God use this person?
- What can we learn from him/her?
- How can I apply their story to my own life?

THIS WEEK I'M PRAYING FOR...

_____
_____
_____
_____
_____
_____
_____

Draw what you think this person looked like.

WEEK 6

Jacob

MEMORY VERSE

"Your name will no longer be Jacob, but Israel, because you have struggled with God and with humans and have overcome." -Genesis 32:28

☐ Day 1- Genesis 31:1-21

- What I learned _____

_____

☐ Day 2- Genesis 31:22-55

- What I learned _____

_____

☐ Day 3- Genesis 32:1-32

- What I learned _____

_____

☐ Day 4- Genesis 33:1-20

- What I learned _____

_____

☐ Day 5- Genesis 35:16-26

- What I learned _____

_____

WEEKEND WRAP UP

This week I will serve or share Jesus with...

_____

- Think of 3 Facts about our person of the week.
- How did God use this person?
- What can we learn from him/her?
- How can I apply their story to my own life?

THIS WEEK I'M PRAYING FOR...

_____
_____
_____
_____
_____
_____
_____

Draw what you think this person looked like.

WEEK 7

Joseph

MEMORY VERSE
"The LORD was with him and the LORD gave him success in everything he did." -Genesis 39:3

☐ ## Day 1- Genesis 37:1-11
- What I learned _____

_____

☐ ## Day 2- Genesis 37:12-36
- What I learned _____

_____

☐ ## Day 3- Genesis 39:1-23
- What I learned _____

_____

☐ ## Day 4- Genesis 40:1-15
- What I learned _____

_____

☐ ## Day 5- Genesis 40:16-23
- What I learned _____

_____

WEEKEND WRAP UP

This week I will serve or share Jesus with...

_____

- Think of 3 facts about our person of the week.
- How did God use this person?
- What can we learn from him/her?
- How can I apply their story to my own life?

THIS WEEK I'M PRAYING FOR...

_____
_____
_____
_____
_____
_____
_____

Draw what you think this person looked like.

WEEK 8

Joseph

> **MEMORY VERSE**
>
> "And all the world came to Egypt to buy grain from Joseph because the famine was severe everywhere."
> -Genesis 41:57

☐ **Day 1- Genesis 41:1-14**
  - What I learned _____

    _____

☐ **Day 2- Genesis 41:15-40**
  - What I learned _____

    _____

☐ **Day 3- Genesis 41:41-57**
  - What I learned _____

    _____

☐ **Day 4- Genesis 42:1-20**
  - What I learned _____

    _____

☐ **Day 5- Genesis 42:21-38**
  - What I learned _____

    _____

WEEKEND WRAP UP

This week I will serve or share Jesus with...

_____

- Think of 3 facts about our person of the week.
- How did God use this person?
- What can we learn from him/her?
- How can I apply their story to my own life?

THIS WEEK I'M PRAYING FOR...

_____
_____
_____
_____
_____
_____
_____

Draw what you think this person looked like.

WEEK 9

Joseph

MEMORY VERSE
"So then it was not you who sent me here, but God. He made me father to Pharaoh, lord of his entire household and ruler of all Egypt." -Genesis 45:8

☐ **Day 1- Genesis 43:1-14**
  - What I learned _____

    _____

☐ **Day 2- Genesis 43:15-34**
  - What I learned _____

    _____

☐ **Day 3- Genesis 44:1-34**
  - What I learned _____

    _____

☐ **Day 4- Genesis 45:1-28**
  - What I learned _____

    _____

☐ **Day 5- Genesis 47:1-12**
  - What I learned _____

    _____

WEEKEND WRAP UP

This week I will serve or share Jesus with...

_____

- Think of 3 Facts about our person of the week.
- How did God use this person?
- What can we learn from him/her?
- How can I apply their story to my own life?

THIS WEEK I'M PRAYING FOR...

_____
_____
_____
_____
_____
_____
_____

Draw what you think this person looked like.

WEEK 10

Moses

> ### MEMORY VERSE
> "I will help you speak and will teach you what to say."
> -Exodus 4:12

☐ ## Day 1- Exodus 1:6-22
- What I learned _____
_____

☐ ## Day 2- Exodus 2:1-10
- What I learned _____
_____

☐ ## Day 3- Exodus 2:11-25
- What I learned _____
_____

☐ ## Day 4- Exodus 3:1-22
- What I learned _____
_____

☐ ## Day 5- Exodus 4:1-17
- What I learned _____
_____

WEEKEND WRAP UP

This week I will serve or share Jesus with...

_____

- Think of 3 Facts about our person of the week.
- How did God use this person?
- What can we learn from him/her?
- How can I apply their story to my own life?

THIS WEEK I'M PRAYING FOR...

_____
_____
_____
_____
_____
_____
_____

Draw what you think this person looked like.

WEEK 11

Moses

> ### MEMORY VERSE
>
> "But the LORD hardened Pharaoh's heart, and he was not willing to let them go." -Exodus 10:27

☐ ### Day 1- Exodus 6:28-30; 7:1-24
  - What I learned _____

    _____

☐ ### Day 2- Exodus 8:1-15
  - What I learned _____

    _____

☐ ### Day 3- Exodus 8:16-32
  - What I learned _____

    _____

☐ ### Day 4- Exodus 9:1-12
  - What I learned _____

    _____

☐ ### Day 5- Exodus 9:13-35
  - What I learned _____

    _____

WEEKEND WRAP UP

This week I will serve or share Jesus with...

_____

- Think of 3 Facts about our person of the week.
- How did God use this person?
- What can we learn from him/her?
- How can I apply their story to my own life?

THIS WEEK I'M PRAYING FOR...

_____

_____

_____

_____

_____

_____

_____

Draw what you think this person looked like.

WEEK 12

Moses

> **MEMORY VERSE**
>
> "The LORD is my strength and my defense."
> -Exodus 15:2

☐ ## Day 1- Exodus 10:1-29

- What I learned _____

_____

☐ ## Day 2- Exodus 12:1-30

- What I learned _____

_____

☐ ## Day 3- Exodus 12:31-42

- What I learned _____

_____

☐ ## Day 4- Exodus 13:17-22; 14:1-12

- What I learned _____

_____

☐ ## Day 5- Exodus 14:13-31

- What I learned _____

_____

WEEKEND WRAP UP

This week I will serve or share Jesus with...

_____

- Think of 3 Facts about our person of the week.
- How did God use this person?
- What can we learn from him/her?
- How can I apply their story to my own life?

THIS WEEK I'M PRAYING FOR...

_____
_____
_____
_____
_____
_____
_____

Draw what you think this person looked like.

WEEK 13

Joshua

> ### MEMORY VERSE
> "Be strong and courageous. Do not be terrified; do not be discouraged, for the Lord your God will be with you wherever you go." -Joshua 1:9

☐ ### Day 1- Joshua 1:1-18
- What I learned _____
_____

☐ ### Day 2- Joshua 2:1-24
- What I learned _____
_____

☐ ### Day 3- Joshua 5:13-15; 6:1-5
- What I learned _____
_____

☐ ### Day 4- Joshua 6:6-14
- What I learned _____
_____

☐ ### Day 5- Joshua 6:15-27
- What I learned _____
_____

WEEKEND WRAP UP

This week I will serve or share Jesus with...

_____

- Think of 3 facts about our person of the week.
- How did God use this person?
- What can we learn from him/her?
- How can I apply their story to my own life?

THIS WEEK I'M PRAYING FOR...

_____
_____
_____
_____
_____
_____
_____

Draw what you think this person looked like.

WEEK 14

date

Deborah and Gideon

MEMORY VERSE
"I will sing to the LORD; I will praise the LORD, the God of Israel in song." -Judges 5:3

☐ **Day 1- Judges 4:1-24**
- What I learned _____
_____

☐ **Day 2- Judges 5:1-31**
- What I learned _____
_____

☐ **Day 3- Judges 6:1-18**
- What I learned _____
_____

☐ **Day 4- Judges 6:19-40**
- What I learned _____
_____

☐ **Day 5- Judges 7:1-25**
- What I learned _____
_____

WEEKEND WRAP UP

This week I will serve or share Jesus with...

_____

- Think of 3 Facts about our person of the week.
- How did God use this person?
- What can we learn from him/her?
- How can I apply their story to my own life?

THIS WEEK I'M PRAYING FOR...

_____
_____
_____
_____
_____
_____
_____

Draw what you think this person looked like.

WEEK 15

Samson

MEMORY VERSE
"You will become pregnant and have a son whose head is never to be touched by a razor. He will take the lead in delivering Israel from the hands of the Philistines."
-Judges 13:5

☐ ## Day 1- Judges 13:1-7; 24-25

- What I learned _____

_____

☐ ## Day 2- Judges 14:1-20

- What I learned _____

_____

☐ ## Day 3- Judges 15:1-20

- What I learned _____

_____

☐ ## Day 4- Judges 16:1-16

- What I learned _____

_____

☐ ## Day 5- Judges 16:17-31

- What I learned _____

_____

WEEKEND WRAP UP

This week I will serve or share Jesus with...

_____

- Think of 3 Facts about our person of the week.
- How did God use this person?
- What can we learn from him/her?
- How can I apply their story to my own life?

THIS WEEK I'M PRAYING FOR...

_____
_____
_____
_____
_____
_____
_____

Draw what you think this person looked like.

WEEK 16

Ruth

MEMORY VERSE
"Where you go I will go, and where you stay I will stay. Your people will be my people and your God my God."
-Ruth 1:16

☐ **Day 1- Ruth 1:1-22**
- What I learned _____
_____

☐ **Day 2- Ruth 2:1-13**
- What I learned _____
_____

☐ **Day 3- Ruth 2:14-23**
- What I learned _____
_____

☐ **Day 4- Ruth 3:1-18**
- What I learned _____
_____

☐ **Day 5- Ruth 4:1-22**
- What I learned _____
_____

WEEKEND WRAP UP

This week I will serve or share Jesus with...

_____

- Think of 3 facts about our person of the week.
- How did God use this person?
- What can we learn from him/her?
- How can I apply their story to my own life?

THIS WEEK I'M PRAYING FOR...

_____
_____
_____
_____
_____
_____
_____

Draw what you think this person looked like.

WEEK 17

Hannah and Samuel

MEMORY VERSE
"I prayed for this child, and the LORD has granted me what I asked of him." -1 Samuel 1:27

☐ ## Day 1- 1 Samuel 1:1-20
- What I learned _____
_____

☐ ## Day 2- 1 Samuel 1:21-28
- What I learned _____
_____

☐ ## Day 3- 1 Samuel 2:1-11
- What I learned _____
_____

☐ ## Day 4- 1 Samuel 3:1-21
- What I learned _____
_____

☐ ## Day 5- 1 Samuel 8:1-22
- What I learned _____
_____

WEEKEND WRAP UP

This week I will serve or share Jesus with...

_____

- Think of 3 facts about our person of the week.
- How did God use this person?
- What can we learn from him/her?
- How can I apply their story to my own life?

THIS WEEK I'M PRAYING FOR...

_____
_____
_____
_____
_____
_____
_____

Draw what you think this person looked like.

WEEK 18

Samuel

> ### MEMORY VERSE
> "To obey is better than sacrifice."
> -1 Samuel 15:22

☐ **Day 1- 1 Samuel 9:1-14**

▪ What I learned _____

_____

☐ **Day 2- 1 Samuel 9:15-27; 10:1-8**

▪ What I learned _____

_____

☐ **Day 3- 1 Samuel 12:1-25**

▪ What I learned _____

_____

☐ **Day 4- 1 Samuel 13:1-15**

▪ What I learned _____

_____

☐ **Day 5- 1 Samuel 16:1-13**

▪ What I learned _____

_____

WEEKEND WRAP UP

This week I will serve or share Jesus with...

_____

- Think of 3 Facts about our person of the week.
- How did God use this person?
- What can we learn from him/her?
- How can I apply their story to my own life?

THIS WEEK I'M PRAYING FOR...

_____
_____
_____
_____
_____
_____
_____

Draw what you think this person looked like.

WEEK 19

Saul and David

> **MEMORY VERSE**
> "People look at the outward appearance, but the LORD looks at the heart." -1 Samuel 16:7

☐ **Day 1- 1 Samuel 10:9-27**
  - What I learned _____
    _____

☐ **Day 2- 1 Samuel 11:1-15**
  - What I learned _____
    _____

☐ **Day 3- 1 Samuel 15:1-19**
  - What I learned _____
    _____

☐ **Day 4- 1 Samuel 15:20-35**
  - What I learned _____
    _____

☐ **Day 5- 1 Samuel 16:14-23**
  - What I learned _____
    _____

WEEKEND WRAP UP

This week I will serve or share Jesus with...

_____

- Think of 3 Facts about our person of the week.
- How did God use this person?
- What can we learn from him/her?
- How can I apply their story to my own life?

THIS WEEK I'M PRAYING FOR...

_____
_____
_____
_____
_____
_____
_____

Draw what you think this person looked like.

WEEK 20

Saul and David

MEMORY VERSE
"The LORD who rescued me from the paw of the lion and the paw of the bear will rescue me from the hand of this Philistine." -1 Samuel 17:37

☐ Day 1- 1 Samuel 17:1-27
  ■ What I learned _____

  _____

☐ Day 2- 1 Samuel 17:28-58
  ■ What I learned _____

  _____

☐ Day 3- 1 Samuel 18:1-11
  ■ What I learned _____

  _____

☐ Day 4- 1 Samuel 18:12-30
  ■ What I learned _____

  _____

☐ Day 5- 1 Samuel 19:1-24
  ■ What I learned _____

  _____

WEEKEND WRAP UP

This week I will serve or share Jesus with...

_____

- Think of 3 facts about our person of the week.
- How did God use this person?
- What can we learn from him/her?
- How can I apply their story to my own life?

THIS WEEK I'M PRAYING FOR...

_____
_____
_____
_____
_____
_____
_____

Draw what you think this person looked like.

WEEK 21

date

Saul, Jonathan, and David

MEMORY VERSE

"The LORD will do what is good in his sight."
-2 Samuel 10:12

☐ **Day 1- 1 Samuel 20:1-23**

- What I learned _____

_____

☐ **Day 2- 1 Samuel 20:24-42**

- What I learned _____

_____

☐ **Day 3- 1 Samuel 23:1-6**

- What I learned _____

_____

☐ **Day 4- 1 Samuel 23:7-29**

- What I learned _____

_____

☐ **Day 5- 1 Samuel 24:1-22**

- What I learned _____

_____

WEEKEND WRAP UP

This week I will serve or share Jesus with...

_____

- Think of 3 Facts about our person of the week.
- How did God use this person?
- What can we learn from him/her?
- How can I apply their story to my own life?

THIS WEEK I'M PRAYING FOR...

_____
_____
_____
_____
_____
_____
_____

Draw what you think this person looked like.

WEEK 22

David and Bathsheba

MEMORY VERSE
"Truly my soul finds rest in God; my salvation comes from him. Truly he is my rock and my salvation; he is my fortress, I will never be shaken." -Psalm 62:1-2

☐ **Day 1- 2 Samuel 11:1-13**
- What I learned _____
_____

☐ **Day 2- 2 Samuel 11:14-27**
- What I learned _____
_____

☐ **Day 3- 2 Samuel 12:1-10**
- What I learned _____
_____

☐ **Day 4- 2 Samuel 12:11-18**
- What I learned _____
_____

☐ **Day 5- 2 Samuel 12:19-25**
- What I learned _____
_____

WEEKEND WRAP UP

This week I will serve or share Jesus with...

_____

- Think of 3 Facts about our person of the week.
- How did God use this person?
- What can we learn from him/her?
- How can I apply their story to my own life?

THIS WEEK I'M PRAYING FOR...

_____

_____

_____

_____

_____

_____

_____

Draw what you think this person looked like.

WEEK 23

Solomon

MEMORY VERSE
"LORD, the God of Israel, there is no God like you in heaven above or on earth below." -1 Kings 8:23

☐ Day 1- 2 Samuel 12:24; 1 Kings 1:28-35
- What I learned _____
_____

☐ Day 2- 1 Kings 2:1-12
- What I learned _____
_____

☐ Day 3- 1 Kings 3:1-15
- What I learned _____
_____

☐ Day 4- 1 Kings 3:16-28
- What I learned _____
_____

☐ Day 5- 1 Kings 4:29-34
- What I learned _____
_____

WEEKEND WRAP UP

This week I will serve or share Jesus with...

_____

- Think of 3 Facts about our person of the week.
- How did God use this person?
- What can we learn from him/her?
- How can I apply their story to my own life?

THIS WEEK I'M PRAYING FOR...

_____
_____
_____
_____
_____
_____
_____

Draw what you think this person looked like.

WEEK 24

Elijah

MEMORY VERSE
"Now I know that you are a man of God and that the word of the LORD from your mouth is the truth."
-1 Kings 17:24

☐ Day 1- 1 Kings 17:1-24

- What I learned _____

_____

☐ Day 2- 1 Kings 18:1-15

- What I learned _____

_____

☐ Day 3- 1 Kings 18:16-46

- What I learned _____

_____

☐ Day 4- 1 Kings 19:1-21

- What I learned _____

_____

☐ Day 5- 2 Kings 1:1-18

- What I learned _____

_____

WEEKEND WRAP UP

This week I will serve or share Jesus with...

_____

- Think of 3 Facts about our person of the week.
- How did God use this person?
- What can we learn from him/her?
- How can I apply their story to my own life?

THIS WEEK I'M PRAYING FOR...

_____
_____
_____
_____
_____
_____
_____

Draw what you think this person looked like.

WEEK 25

Elisha

> **MEMORY VERSE**
> "You alone are God over all the kingdoms of the earth. You have made heaven and earth."
> -2 Kings 19:15

☐ ### Day 1- 2 Kings 2:1-18
- What I learned _____
_____

☐ ### Day 2- 2 Kings 2:19-25
- What I learned _____
_____

☐ ### Day 3- 2 Kings 4:1-7
- What I learned _____
_____

☐ ### Day 4- 2 Kings 4:8-37
- What I learned _____
_____

☐ ### Day 5- 2 Kings 5:1-15
- What I learned _____
_____

WEEKEND WRAP UP

This week I will serve or share Jesus with...

_____

- Think of 3 Facts about our person of the week.
- How did God use this person?
- What can we learn from him/her?
- How can I apply their story to my own life?

THIS WEEK I'M PRAYING FOR...

_____
_____
_____
_____
_____
_____
_____

Draw what you think this person looked like.

WEEK 26

Esther

> MEMORY VERSE
> "And who knows but that you have come to your royal position for such a time as this?"
> -Esther 4:14

☐ Day 1- Esther 2:1-23
- What I learned _____

_____

☐ Day 2- Esther 3:1-15
- What I learned _____

_____

☐ Day 3- Esther 4:1-17
- What I learned _____

_____

☐ Day 4- Esther 5:1-14
- What I learned _____

_____

☐ Day 5- Esther 6:1-14; 7:1-10
- What I learned _____

_____

WEEKEND WRAP UP

This week I will serve or share Jesus with...

_____

- Think of 3 Facts about our person of the week.
- How did God use this person?
- What can we learn from him/her?
- How can I apply their story to my own life?

THIS WEEK I'M PRAYING FOR...

_____
_____
_____
_____
_____
_____
_____

Draw what you think this person looked like.

WEEK 27

Job

> **MEMORY VERSE**
> "God's voice thunders in marvelous ways; he does great things beyond our understanding."
> -Job 37:5

☐ **Day 1- Job 1:1-22**
- What I learned _____
_____

☐ **Day 2- Job 2:1-13**
- What I learned _____
_____

☐ **Day 3- Job 39:1-12**
- What I learned _____
_____

☐ **Day 4- Job 39:13-30**
- What I learned _____
_____

☐ **Day 5- Job 42:1-17**
- What I learned _____
_____

WEEKEND WRAP UP

This week I will serve or share Jesus with...

_____

- Think of 3 Facts about our person of the week.
- How did God use this person?
- What can we learn from him/her?
- How can I apply their story to my own life?

THIS WEEK I'M PRAYING FOR...

_____
_____
_____
_____
_____
_____
_____

Draw what you think this person looked like.

WEEK 28

date

Daniel/ Shadrach, Meshach, and Abednego

MEMORY VERSE
"Praise be to the name of God for ever and ever."
-Daniel 2:20

☐ ## Day 1- Daniel 1:1-21
- What I learned _____
_____

☐ ## Day 2- Daniel 2:1-23
- What I learned _____
_____

☐ ## Day 3- Daniel 2:24-49
- What I learned _____
_____

☐ ## Day 4- Daniel 3:1-23
- What I learned _____
_____

☐ ## Day 5-Daniel 3:24-30
- What I learned _____
_____

WEEKEND WRAP UP

This week I will serve or share Jesus with...

_____

- Think of 3 Facts about our person of the week.
- How did God use this person?
- What can we learn from him/her?
- How can I apply their story to my own life?

THIS WEEK I'M PRAYING FOR...

_____

_____

_____

_____

_____

_____

_____

Draw what you think this person looked like.

WEEK 29

Daniel

> **MEMORY VERSE**
>
> "Surely your God is the God of gods and the Lord of kings."
> -Daniel 2:47

☐ **Day 1- Daniel 4:1-18**
- What I learned _____
  _____

☐ **Day 2- Daniel 4:19-37**
- What I learned _____
  _____

☐ **Day 3- Daniel 5:1-30**
- What I learned _____
  _____

☑ **Day 4- Daniel 6:1-16**
- What I learned Daniel prayed so he got thrown into the lions den.

☐ **Day 5- Daniel 6:17-28**
- What I learned God resuced Daniel and the king therw the 3 men in the lions den along with there family.

WEEKEND WRAP UP

This week I will serve or share Jesus with...

My Mom

- Think of 3 facts about our person of the week.
- How did God use this person?
- What can we learn from him/her?
- How can I apply their story to my own life?

Draw what you think this person looked like.

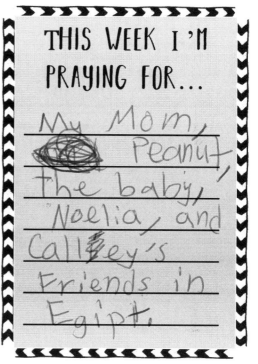

THIS WEEK I'M PRAYING FOR...

My Mom, Peanut, the baby, Noelia, and Callbey's friends in Egipt.

WEEK 30

Jonah

> ### MEMORY VERSE
> "And the LORD commanded the fish, and it vomited Jonah onto dry land." -Jonah 2:10

☐ ## Day 1- Jonah 1:1-10
   - What I learned _____
   _____

☐ ## Day 2- Jonah 1:11-17
   - What I learned _____
   _____

☐ ## Day 3- Jonah 2:1-10
   - What I learned _____
   _____

☐ ## Day 4- Jonah 3:1-10
   - What I learned _____
   _____

☐ ## Day 5- Jonah 4:1-11
   - What I learned _____
   _____

WEEKEND WRAP UP

This week I will serve or share Jesus with...

_____

- Think of 3 facts about our person of the week.
- How did God use this person?
- What can we learn from him/her?
- How can I apply their story to my own life?

THIS WEEK I'M PRAYING FOR...

_____

_____

_____

_____

_____

_____

_____

Draw what you think this person looked like.

WEEK 31

Psalm

MEMORY VERSE

"Your word is a lamp for my feet, a light on my path."
-Psalm 119:105

☐ ### Day 1- Psalm 1
- What I learned _____
_____

☐ ### Day 2- Psalm 19
- What I learned _____
_____

☐ ### Day 3- Psalm 23
- What I learned _____
_____

☐ ### Day 4- Psalm 34
- What I learned _____
_____

☐ ### Day 5- Psalm 121
- What I learned _____
_____

WEEKEND WRAP UP

This week I will serve or share Jesus with...

_____

- Think of 3 facts about our person of the week.
- How did God use this person?
- What can we learn from him/her?
- How can I apply their story to my own life?

THIS WEEK I'M PRAYING FOR...

_____
_____
_____
_____
_____
_____
_____

Draw what you think this person looked like.

WEEK 32

Proverbs

MEMORY VERSE
"Trust in the LORD with all your heart and lean not on your own understanding; in all your ways submit to him, and he will make your paths straight."
-Proverbs 3:5-6

☐ **Day 1- Proverbs 3:1-6**
- What I learned _____
_____

☐ **Day 2- Proverbs 4:20-27**
- What I learned _____
_____

☐ **Day 3- Proverbs 10:1-8**
- What I learned _____
_____

☐ **Day 4- Proverbs 13:1-3**
- What I learned _____
_____

☐ **Day 5- Proverbs 22:1-6**
- What I learned _____
_____

WEEKEND WRAP UP

This week I will serve or share Jesus with...

_____

- Think of 3 Facts about our person of the week.
- How did God use this person?
- What can we learn from him/her?
- How can I apply their story to my own life?

THIS WEEK I'M PRAYING FOR...

_____

_____

_____

_____

_____

_____

_____

Draw what you think this person looked like.

WEEK 33

John the Baptist

> **MEMORY VERSE**
> "I am the voice of one calling in the wilderness, Make
> straight the way for the Lord."
> -John 1:23

☐ **Day 1- Luke 1:5-25**
- What I learned _____
  _____

☐ **Day 2- Luke 1:57-66; 80**
- What I learned _____
  _____

☐ **Day 3- Matthew 3:1-17**
- What I learned _____
  _____

☐ **Day 4- Luke 3:1-20**
- What I learned _____
  _____

☐ **Day 5- John 1:19-34**
- What I learned _____
  _____

WEEKEND WRAP UP

This week I will serve or share Jesus with...

_____

- Think of 3 facts about our person of the week.
- How did God use this person?
- What can we learn from him/her?
- How can I apply their story to my own life?

THIS WEEK I'M PRAYING FOR...

_____
_____
_____
_____
_____
_____
_____

Draw what you think this person looked like.

WEEK 34

Joseph and Mary

> **MEMORY VERSE**
> "My soul glorifies the Lord and my spirit rejoices in God my Savior." -Luke 1:46-47

☐ **Day 1- Luke 1:26-45**
- What I learned _____
  _____

☐ **Day 2- Luke 1:46-56**
- What I learned _____
  _____

☐ **Day 3- Matthew 1:18-25**
- What I learned _____
  _____

☐ **Day 4- Luke 2:22-40**
- What I learned _____
  _____

☐ **Day 5- Luke 2:41-52**
- What I learned _____
  _____

WEEKEND WRAP UP

This week I will serve or share Jesus with...

_____

- Think of 3 facts about our person of the week.
- How did God use this person?
- What can we learn from him/her?
- How can I apply their story to my own life?

THIS WEEK I'M PRAYING FOR...

_____
_____
_____
_____
_____
_____
_____

Draw what you think this person looked like.

WEEK 35

The birth of Jesus

MEMORY VERSE

"For the law was given through Moses; grace and truth came through Jesus Christ." -John 1:17

☐ Day 1- Luke 2:1-12
- What I learned _____
_____

☐ Day 2- Luke 2:13-21
- What I learned _____
_____

☐ Day 3- Matthew 2:1-12
- What I learned _____
_____

☐ Day 4- Matthew 2:13-18
- What I learned _____
_____

☐ Day 5- Matthew 2:19-23
- What I learned _____
_____

WEEKEND WRAP UP

This week I will serve or share Jesus with...

_____

- Think of 3 facts about our person of the week.
- How did God use this person?
- What can we learn from him/her?
- How can I apply their story to my own life?

THIS WEEK I'M PRAYING FOR...

_____
_____
_____
_____
_____
_____
_____

Draw what you think this person looked like.

WEEK 36

Jesus in the book of Matthew

MEMORY VERSE
"You are the light of the world." -Matthew 5:14

☐ **Day 1- Matthew 5:1-12**
- What I learned _____
_____

☐ **Day 2- Matthew 14:13-21**
- What I learned _____
_____

☐ **Day 3- Matthew 14:22-36**
- What I learned _____
_____

☐ **Day 4- Matthew 18:10-14**
- What I learned _____
_____

☐ **Day 5- Matthew 21:1-11**
- What I learned _____
_____

WEEKEND WRAP UP

This week I will serve or share Jesus with...

_____

- Think of 3 Facts about our person of the week.
- How did God use this person?
- What can we learn from him/her?
- How can I apply their story to my own life?

THIS WEEK I'M PRAYING FOR...

_____
_____
_____
_____
_____
_____
_____

Draw what you think this person looked like.

WEEK 37

Jesus in the book of Mark

MEMORY VERSE
"Love the Lord your God with all your heart and with all your heart and with all your soul and with all your mind and with all your strength."
-Mark 12:30

☐ **Day 1- Mark 2:1-12**
- What I learned _____

_____

☐ **Day 2- Mark 4:35-41**
- What I learned _____

_____

☐ **Day 3- Mark 5:21-43**
- What I learned _____

_____

☐ **Day 4- Mark 6:45-56**
- What I learned _____

_____

☐ **Day 5- Mark 10:17-31**
- What I learned _____

_____

WEEKEND WRAP UP

This week I will serve or share Jesus with...

_____

- Think of 3 facts about our person of the week.
- How did God use this person?
- What can we learn from him/her?
- How can I apply their story to my own life?

THIS WEEK I'M PRAYING FOR...

_____
_____
_____
_____
_____
_____
_____

Draw what you think this person looked like.

WEEK 38

date

Jesus in the book of Luke

> **MEMORY VERSE**
> "Ask and it will be given to you; seek and you will find;
> knock and the door will be opened to you."
> -Luke 11:9

☐ ## Day 1- Luke 7:11-17
  - What I learned _____
  _____

☐ ## Day 2- Luke 16:19-31
  - What I learned _____
  _____

☐ ## Day 3- Luke 17:11-19
  - What I learned _____
  _____

☐ ## Day 4- Luke 18:9-14
  - What I learned _____
  _____

☐ ## Day 5- Luke 19:1-10
  - What I learned _____
  _____

WEEKEND WRAP UP

This week I will serve or share Jesus with...

_____

- Think of 3 Facts about our person of the week.
- How did God use this person?
- What can we learn from him/her?
- How can I apply their story to my own life?

THIS WEEK I'M PRAYING FOR...

_____
_____
_____
_____
_____
_____
_____

Draw what you think this person looked like.

WEEK 39

Jesus in the book of John

> **MEMORY VERSE**
> "For God so loved the world that he gave his one and only Son, that whoever believes in him shall not perish but have eternal life." -John 3:16

☐ **Day 1- John 2:1-11**
- What I learned _____
_____

☐ **Day 2- John 4:1-26**
- What I learned _____
_____

☐ **Day 3- John 9:1-12**
- What I learned _____
_____

☐ **Day 4- John 13:1-17**
- What I learned _____
_____

☐ **Day 5- John 17:6-19**
- What I learned _____
_____

WEEKEND WRAP UP

This week I will serve or share Jesus with...

_____

- Think of 3 Facts about our person of the week.
- How did God use this person?
- What can we learn from him/her?
- How can I apply their story to my own life?

THIS WEEK I'M PRAYING FOR...

_____
_____
_____
_____
_____
_____
_____

Draw what you think this person looked like.

WEEK 40

Parables of Jesus

MEMORY VERSE

"But while he was still a long way off, his father saw him and was filled with compassion for him; he ran to his son, threw his arms around him and kissed him." -Luke 15:20

☐ ## Day 1- Luke 10:25-37

- What I learned _____

_____

☐ ## Day 2- Luke 8:1-15

- What I learned _____

_____

☐ ## Day 3- Luke 15:1-10

- What I learned _____

_____

☐ ## Day 4- Luke 15:11-32

- What I learned _____

_____

☐ ## Day 5- Luke 6:46-49

- What I learned _____

_____

WEEKEND WRAP UP

This week I will serve or share Jesus with...

_____

- Think of 3 facts about our person of the week.
- How did God use this person?
- What can we learn from him/her?
- How can I apply their story to my own life?

THIS WEEK I'M PRAYING FOR...

_____
_____
_____
_____
_____
_____
_____

Draw what you think this person looked like.

WEEK 41

Jesus- life and ministry

MEMORY VERSE
"Let the little children come to me, and do not hinder them, for the kingdom of heaven belongs to such as these."
-Matthew 19:14

☐ ## Day 1- Luke 4:1-13

- What I learned _____

_____

☐ ## Day 2- Luke 5:1-11; 6:12-15

- What I learned _____

_____

☐ ## Day 3- Mark 11:12-26

- What I learned _____

_____

☐ ## Day 4- Matthew 19:13-15; Mark 10:13-16

- What I learned _____

_____

☐ ## Day 5- Luke 11:1-13

- What I learned _____

_____

WEEKEND WRAP UP

This week I will serve or share Jesus with...

_____

- Think of 3 Facts about our person of the week.
- How did God use this person?
- What can we learn from him/her?
- How can I apply their story to my own life?

THIS WEEK I'M PRAYING FOR...

_____
_____
_____
_____
_____
_____
_____

Draw what you think this person looked like.

WEEK 42

Jesus- life and ministry

> **MEMORY VERSE**
> "Do to others as you would have them do to you."
> -Luke 6:31

☐ **Day 1- John 1:1-17**
- What I learned _____
  _____

☐ **Day 2- Matthew 18:10-14**
- What I learned _____
  _____

☐ **Day 3- Mark 12:41-44**
- What I learned _____
  _____

☐ **Day 4- Matthew 22:34-40**
- What I learned _____
  _____

☐ **Day 5- Luke 6:27-42**
- What I learned _____
  _____

WEEKEND WRAP UP

This week I will serve or share Jesus with...

_____

- Think of 3 facts about our person of the week.
- How did God use this person?
- What can we learn from him/her?
- How can I apply their story to my own life?

THIS WEEK I'M PRAYING FOR...

_____
_____
_____
_____
_____
_____
_____

Draw what you think this person looked like.

WEEK 43

Jesus- death, burial and resurrection

> **MEMORY VERSE**
> "Greater love has no one than this: to lay down one's life
> for one's friends."
> -John 15:13

☐ **Day 1- Matthew 26:17-29**
- What I learned _____
_____

☐ **Day 2- Matthew 26:36-56; Luke 22:47-53**
- What I learned _____
_____

☐ **Day 3- Matthew 27:11-44**
- What I learned _____
_____

☐ **Day 4- Matthew 27:45-66**
- What I learned _____
_____

☐ **Day 5- Mark 16:1-8; John 20:24-31**
- What I learned _____
_____

WEEKEND WRAP UP

This week I will serve or share Jesus with...

_____

- Think of 3 facts about our person of the week.
- How did God use this person?
- What can we learn from him/her?
- How can I apply their story to my own life?

THIS WEEK I'M PRAYING FOR...

_____
_____
_____
_____
_____
_____
_____

Draw what you think this person looked like.

WEEK 44

Mary Magdalene

MEMORY VERSE

"He is not here; He has risen!" -Luke 24:6

☐ **Day 1- Luke 8:1-3**
- What I learned _____
_____

☐ **Day 2- Mark 15:33-41**
- What I learned _____
_____

☐ **Day 3- Mark 16:1-20**
- What I learned _____
_____

☐ **Day 4- Luke 24:1-12**
- What I learned _____
_____

☐ **Day 5- John 20:1-8**
- What I learned _____
_____

WEEKEND WRAP UP

This week I will serve or share Jesus with...

_____

- Think of 3 Facts about our person of the week.
- How did God use this person?
- What can we learn from him/her?
- How can I apply their story to my own life?

THIS WEEK I'M PRAYING FOR...

_____
_____
_____
_____
_____
_____
_____

Draw what you think this person looked like.

WEEK 45

Mary, Martha, and Lazarus

MEMORY VERSE

"Did I not tell you that if you believe, you will see the glory of God?" -John 11:40

☐ **Day 1- John 11:1-16**

■ What I learned _____

_____

☐ **Day 2- John 11:17-37**

■ What I learned _____

_____

☐ **Day 3- John 11:38-44**

■ What I learned _____

_____

☐ **Day 4- John 12:1-11**

■ What I learned _____

_____

☐ **Day 5- Luke 10:38-42**

■ What I learned _____

_____

WEEKEND WRAP UP

This week I will serve or share Jesus with...

_____

- Think of 3 Facts about our person of the week.
- How did God use this person?
- What can we learn from him/her?
- How can I apply their story to my own life?

THIS WEEK I'M PRAYING FOR...

_____
_____
_____
_____
_____
_____
_____

Draw what you think this person looked like.

WEEK 46

Peter

> **MEMORY VERSE**
> "Silver or gold I do not have, but what I do have I give you.
> In the name of Jesus Christ of Nazareth, walk."
> -Acts 3:6

☐ **Day 1- Matthew 14:22-36**
- What I learned _____
_____

☐ **Day 2- Mark 14:27-31; 66-72**
- What I learned _____
_____

☐ **Day 3- Acts 3:1-10**
- What I learned _____
_____

☐ **Day 4- Acts 4:1-22**
- What I learned _____
_____

☐ **Day 5- Acts 9:32-43**
- What I learned _____
_____

WEEKEND WRAP UP

This week I will serve or share Jesus with...

_____

- Think of 3 facts about our person of the week.
- How did God use this person?
- What can we learn from him/her?
- How can I apply their story to my own life?

THIS WEEK I'M PRAYING FOR...

_____

_____

_____

_____

_____

_____

_____

Draw what you think this person looked like.

WEEK 47

Paul

> ### MEMORY VERSE
> "Be kind and compassionate to one another, forgiving each other, just as in Christ God forgave you."
> -Ephesians 4:32

☐ Day 1- Acts 9:1-19
- What I learned _____
_____

☐ Day 2- Acts 9:19-31
- What I learned _____
_____

☐ Day 3- Acts 16:16-40
- What I learned _____
_____

☐ Day 4- Acts 27:1-12
- What I learned _____
_____

☐ Day 5- Acts 27:13-44
- What I learned _____
_____

WEEKEND WRAP UP

This week I will serve or share Jesus with...

_____

- Think of 3 facts about our person of the week.
- How did God use this person?
- What can we learn from him/her?
- How can I apply their story to my own life?

THIS WEEK I'M PRAYING FOR...

_____

_____

_____

_____

_____

_____

_____

Draw what you think this person looked like.

WEEK 48

God the Father

> ### MEMORY VERSE
> "Be strong and courageous. Do not be afraid or terrified because of them, for the LORD your God goes with you; he will never leave you nor forsake you." -Deuteronomy 31:6

☐ **Day 1- Psalm 103:1-12**
- What I learned _____
_____

☐ **Day 2- Psalm 103:13-22**
- What I learned _____
_____

☐ **Day 3- Luke 15:11-32**
- What I learned _____
_____

☐ **Day 4- Romans 8:28-39**
- What I learned _____
_____

☐ **Day 5- 1 John 4:7-21**
- What I learned _____
_____

WEEKEND WRAP UP

This week I will serve or share Jesus with...

_____

- Think of 3 facts about our person of the week.
- How did God use this person?
- What can we learn from him/her?
- How can I apply their story to my own life?

Draw some qualities of God the Father.

THIS WEEK I'M PRAYING FOR...

_____
_____
_____
_____
_____
_____
_____

WEEK 49

God the Son

MEMORY VERSE
"The Son of Man came to seek and save the lost."
-Luke 19:10

☐ ## Day 1- John 3:1-21

▪ What I learned _____

_____

☐ ## Day 2- Mark 10:13-16

▪ What I learned _____

_____

☐ ## Day 3- Galatians 3:26-4:7

▪ What I learned _____

_____

☐ ## Day 4- Colossians 1:15-23

▪ What I learned _____

_____

☐ ## Day 5- Galatians 1:3-4; Philippians 2:5-11

▪ What I learned _____

_____

WEEKEND WRAP UP

This week I will serve or share Jesus with...

_____

- Think of 3 facts about our person of the week.
- How did God use this person?
- What can we learn from him/her?
- How can I apply their story to my own life?

THIS WEEK I'M PRAYING FOR...

_____
_____
_____
_____
_____
_____
_____

Draw some qualities of God the Son.

WEEK 50

God the Holy Spirit

MEMORY VERSE
"But the fruit of the Spirit is love, joy, peace, patience, kindness, goodness, faithfulness, gentleness and self-control. Against such things there is no law.
-Galatians 5:22-23

☐ **Day 1- John 14:15-27**
  ▪ What I learned _____

  _____

☐ **Day 2- John 15:26-27; 16:1-15**
  ▪ What I learned _____

  _____

☐ **Day 3- John 20:19-23**
  ▪ What I learned _____

  _____

☐ **Day 4- Romans 8:1-17**
  ▪ What I learned _____

  _____

☐ **Day 5- Galatians 5:16-26**
  ▪ What I learned _____

  _____

WEEKEND WRAP UP

This week I will serve or share Jesus with...

_____

- Think of 3 facts about our person of the week.
- How did God use this person?
- What can we learn from him/her?
- How can I apply their story to my own life?

THIS WEEK I'M PRAYING FOR...

_____
_____
_____
_____
_____
_____
_____

Draw some qualities of God the Holy Spirit.

WEEK 51

Looking Back

Use these last 2 weeks to look back on the past year and pick some of your own favorite stories. Write the verses and what you liked about the story.

- ☐ **Day 1-**
  - ▪ What I learned _____
    _____

- ☐ **Day 2-**
  - ▪ What I learned _____
    _____

- ☐ **Day 3-**
  - ▪ What I learned _____
    _____

- ☐ **Day 4-**
  - ▪ What I learned _____
    _____

- ☐ **Day 5-**
  - ▪ What I learned _____
    _____

WEEKEND WRAP UP

This week I will serve or share Jesus with...

_____

Think of 3 Facts about our person of the week.

• How did God use this person?

• What can we learn from him/her?

• How can I apply their story to my own life?

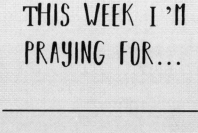

THIS WEEK I'M PRAYING FOR...

_____
_____
_____
_____
_____
_____
_____

Draw a picture to help you remember your favorite story.

WEEK 52

Looking Back

Use these last 2 weeks to look back on the past year and pick some of your own favorite stories. Write the verses and what you liked about the story.

☐ **Day 1-**
   - What I learned _____
   _____

☐ **Day 2-**
   - What I learned _____
   _____

☐ **Day 3-**
   - What I learned _____
   _____

☐ **Day 4-**
   - What I learned _____
   _____

☐ **Day 5-**
   - What I learned _____
   _____

WEEKEND WRAP UP

This week I will serve or share Jesus with...

_____

- Think of 3 facts about our person of the week.
- How did God use this person?
- What can we learn from him/her?
- How can I apply their story to my own life?

THIS WEEK I'M PRAYING FOR...

_____
_____
_____
_____
_____
_____
_____

Draw a picture to help you remember your favorite story.

71587214R00061

Made in the USA
Columbia, SC
01 June 2017